START-UP
ART AND DESIGN

CAN BUILDINGS SPEAK?

Louise and Richard Spilsbury

Evans

Published by Evans Brothers Limited
2A Portman Mansions
Chiltern Street
London W1U 6NR

© Evans Brothers Limited 2007

Produced for Evans Brothers Limited by
White-Thomson Publishing Ltd.
Bridgewater Business Centre, 210 High Street,
Lewes, East Sussex BN7 2NH

Printed in China by WKT Co. Ltd.

Editor: Rachel Minay
Consultant: Susan Ogier Horwood, Art Education
Consultant specialising in Early Years and
Primary age range
Designer: Leishman Design

British Library Cataloguing in Publication Data
Spilsbury, Louise and Richard
    Can buildings speak? - (Start up art and design)
    1. Decoration and ornament, Architectural
    I. Title II. Spilsbury, Richard, 1963-
    729

ISBN-13: 9780237533991

Acknowledgements:
Special thanks to Ms J. Arundell and pupils at Mayfield
Primary School, Hanwell, West London, and Mrs J.
Heath and pupils at Malborough and South Huish
Primary School, South Devon, for their help and
involvement in the preparation of this book.

Picture Acknowledgements:
Alamy pp. 4br (Jim Wileman), 5r (Alan Curtis), 6
(Duncan Hale-Sutton), 12l (Ros Drinkwater); Corbis
pp. cover main (inset) (Gabe Palmer/zefa), 5l (Gillian
Darley; Edifice), 16r (Massimo Listri); Chris Fairclough
pp. title page, 6 (inset), 8 (all), 9b, 11, 13, 17l&r; Jackie
Heath pp. cover tr, 18l, 19l&r, 20 (all); iStockphoto.com
pp. cover main, 4tl, 4tc, 4tr, 4bl, 4bc, 5l (inset), 5r (inset),
14l&r, 16l, 18r; Louise Spilsbury p. 21.

Artwork:
Pupils at Mayfield Primary School, Hanwell, West
London pp. cover tl, 7, 15 (all); Rachel Minay p. 9t (all);
Louise Spilsbury p. 10.

Contents

How buildings speak

Buildings have different uses and purposes. The exterior of a building often tells us what it is for. Can you match these buildings to the words?

House   Railway Station   Theatre

Hospital   Church   Beach Hut

purposes   exterior

The different **features** of a building give us **clues** to its purpose. Windows and doors are features of buildings. What other features can you think of?

"This fire station has big doors so fire engines can get out quickly."

"This leisure centre has lots of large windows to let in natural light."

features   clues

Local buildings

What different types of buildings are in your local area? Are any buildings used for a different purpose from the one they were built for?

"This cinema used to be an office block."

Can you locate some of the different buildings in your area on a local map?

local   locate

Zoe's class **enlarged** a **map** of their local area on the photocopier. They made coloured sketches of local buildings and placed them in the correct locations.

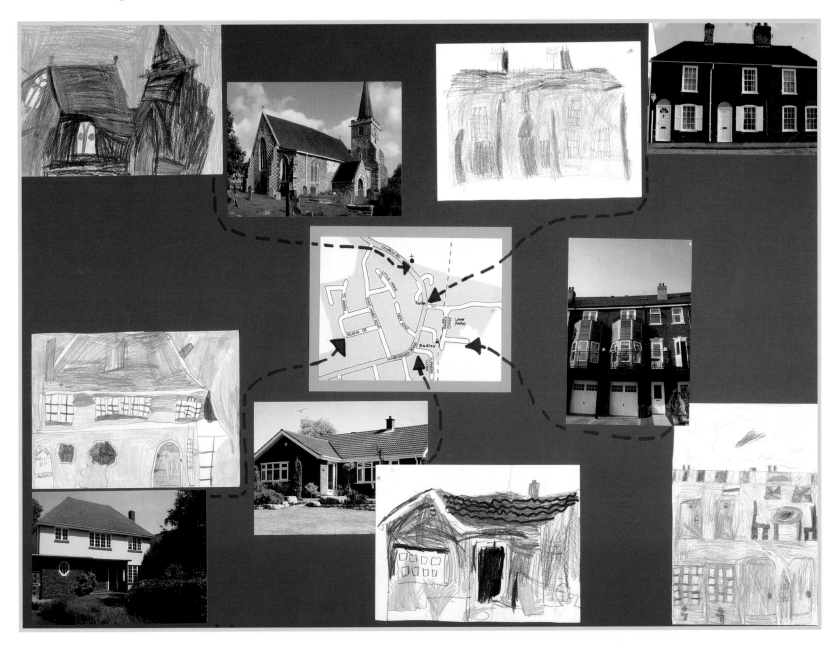

Close-up on school

Sam's class takes close-up photos of patterns on the school building and rubbings of different surfaces.

▶ In class, the children look at the close-up photos on the whiteboard. They try to identify what the patterns are.

patterns   rubbings   surfaces

▼ Some children use the effects tool on the computer to make new patterns from the photos.

 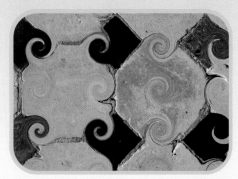 

▶ The patterns give the children ideas for block prints. Maya cuts shapes from polystyrene and sticks them on to a tile. She rolls ink over them. She rotates the prints to make a pattern.

effects   block prints   rotates   9

Making buildings

Buildings are made from different materials. This collage shows what buildings were made of in 1666 when the Great Fire of London happened.

thatched (straw) roofs ...

most houses had .. wooden frames

wooden window frames

wooden .. doors

▲ The fire destroyed most of the city. Which features of the buildings helped the fire spread?

materials   collage   thatched

▼ Ben and his friends collect materials used on and in their homes. They make a display so they can feel the different textures.

glass

plastic

Building Materials

fabric

wood

brick

What materials do you think will be used in houses in the future? Can you draw a design for a future house?

display   textures   design

Public buildings

Public **buildings are those that anyone can visit. Robert's class** explores **a natural history museum. How are the spaces in a public building different from those in a house?**

▶ **The children write** key words **to help them think about the building design.**

How does the building speak to you?

Features: high roof, many windows, wide steps

Spaces: entrance, café, big display rooms

Furniture: benches

Textures: rough brick walls, smooth wooden benches

Shapes: arched roof, square windows

Feelings: peaceful, serious, quiet

Sounds: whispering, footsteps

public   explores   key words

▼ **In class, the children design a banner for the museum on a large cotton sheet. They colour it using fabric paints.**

"The birds and plants in our design are symbols of the natural history museum."

fabric   symbols

Amazing buildings

The architect Antoni Gaudi designed this building. Gaudi was inspired by nature. How would you describe the lines and shapes on the building?

▲ Gaudi used many different materials, such as stone, tiles, iron and bricks. He made mosaics from glass.

architect   inspired   mosaics

Design a **fantasy** building in pencil. **Decorate** it with mosaics by tearing coloured paper into pieces or cutting pictures from magazines.

What sort of person might live in your fantasy building?

fantasy   decorate

Building interiors

The insides of buildings give us information too. How are these two interiors different from one another?

What differences can you see in the colours, furniture and style of these two rooms?

interiors   furniture   style

◄ Marta makes a room inside a shoebox. She makes curtains and furniture to scale. Would you have chosen the same colours and shapes as Marta?

▲ Marta shines a torch through a window to light the room.

scale

Brighten up a building

▼ This class wants to make their school entrance more welcoming. An artist talks to them about stained glass.

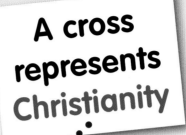
A cross represents Christianity

A dove represents peace

▲ The children visit a church. They look at the symbols in the stained-glass windows.

stained glass   Christianity

▲ The children work together to draw outlines of images that link the school to the surrounding countryside.

► The final design is a combination of everyone's work. What symbols did they use?

Window designs

▼ The children **discuss** which colours to choose from samples of glass.

▼ They cut paper patterns for each piece of coloured glass.

► Why does each shape need to be marked with a different number?

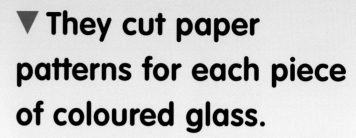

discuss

A **specialist** company makes the window. Do you think the window **improves** the school **environment**?

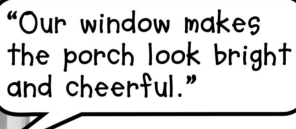

"Our window makes the porch look bright and cheerful."

"I'm so proud that the window will be here for a very long time!"

Further information for

New words listed in the text:

architect	discuss	fantasy	local	purposes	surfaces
block prints	display	features	locate	religious	symbols
Christianity	effects	furniture	map	rotates	textures
clues	enlarged	images	materials	rubbings	thatched
collage	environment	improves	mosaics	scale	
combination	explores	inspired	outlines	specialist	
decorate	exterior	interiors	patterns	stained glass	
design	fabric	key words	public	style	

Possible Activities

PAGES 4-5

Children could look at photos of buildings and discuss features and why buildings have them. Leisure centres have big windows to tempt people in and because natural light makes us feel good when we exercise. Buildings that need to let big vehicles in, like hospitals and stores, have large doors.
Children could make buildings by dragging coloured shapes on screen or using sticky paper shapes for features.

PAGES 6-7

This links with history work about how buildings were in the past and change in use over time. It also fits in with geography work on maps and the local area. Using an enlarged local map, children could trace their routes to school and draw or photograph (for the map) buildings or street furniture that they see on the way.
When sketching a building or detail, children could make their own viewfinder to fix to their clipboard to help them frame a view. See www.tate.org.uk/learning/kids/zoomroom/frameview/

PAGES 8-9

Emphasise here the difference between texture and pattern. Mention that patterns that we observe can be the result of a surface texture. The patterns created by tiles and bricks can link with maths work. For example, are they regular or irregular, symmetrical or geometric?
There are lots of suggestions for geometric pattern activities and templates and designs, for example using circles and stars in borders and tiles at: www.cleavebooks.co.uk/trol/trolna.pdf

PAGES 10-11

At www.firekills.gov.uk/education/teacher/ks2/t2_pdf/t2_great_fire_act.pdf children look at why the fire spread and took a long time to put out. Buildings are safer today because materials and furniture are more likely to be fire resistant, and smoke alarms and sprinkler systems are features of many buildings.
Other buildings from the past to look at could include castles, which have many features that speak to us about their purpose, such as protective drawbridges and high turrets, or Roman amphitheatres and Egyptian pyramids.
The class could write a revised version of 'The Three Little

Parents and Teachers

Pigs', where the three little pigs collaborate on a house design that keeps them all safe from the wolf. This could be written in pairs to reinforce cooperation. They should consider what materials would keep the pigs' house strong and safe.

PAGES 12-13
If possible, arrange a visit to a public building such as a town hall, library or place of worship. Ask how the spaces inside are used and how they tell people the purpose of the building. Do some buildings make us behave in different ways? How and why?

PAGES 14-15
Gaudi (1852–1926) is supposed to have said that only men drew straight lines – God and nature much preferred curves. He took his inspiration from nature, such as rock formations. The curved shapes might make children think of organic forms such as waves or caves.

PAGES 16-17
The children could discuss how the Victorian interior is full of knick-knacks, the walls are papered and there are a lot of rich colours. Victorians felt that a bare room showed poor taste and filled rooms with objects to show they had cultural interests. The modern interior is much lighter, simpler and more uncluttered. Children could discuss what impression the way an interior is decorated and furnished gives.

PAGES 18-19
Stained-glass windows are a feature of churches and children could explore churches and other places of worship for features that tell us what the building is used for.
They could also use tissue paper to make small stained-glass panels for the classroom windows.
Children could identify a part of the school building they could

Further Information

BOOKS FOR CHILDREN
Houses and Homes (Start-Up Design and Technology) by Louise and Richard Spilsbury (Evans, 2005)

Amazing Buildings (DK Readers) by Kate Hayden (Dorling Kindersley, 2003)

Structures, Materials, & Art Activities (Arty Facts) by Barbara Taylor (Crabtree Publishing Company, 2002)

Home (Around the World) by Margaret C Hall (Heinemann Library, 2002)

WEBSITES
http://education.guardian.co.uk/primaryresources/story/0,
,945237,00.html
http://www.tate.org.uk/kids/
http://www.archkidecture.org/

improve and plan a project to brighten it up. This could involve making a temporary mural made from panels with images formed in relief from modroc or clay. Different groups could make a panel each but the set should be designed to work together and ideally represent the school in some way. Or the panels could be made from collage and form a class frieze.

PAGES 20-21
Having an opening for a major project like this or making a special display of children's work is a chance for members of the community to come to the school and engage with the children about their work. Children could act as guides and show visitors around the display, explaining the process and talking about their own and others' work.

Index